# Genealogical Memoranda

RELATING TO THE

FAMILY OF

# JODRELL.

PRIVATELY PRINTED.

1897.

ARMS OF GILBERT SHELDON, D.D., BISHOP OF LONDON,
(AND SUBSEQUENTLY ARCHBISHOP OF CANTERBURY).

*Copied from the original Grant of Arms dated 1660, in the possession of Sir Alfred Jodrell, Bart.*

# Genealogical Memoranda

RELATING TO THE

# Family of Jodrell.

---

## *Grant of Arms to Gilbert Sheldon,*[1] *D.D.*, 1660.

Universis et Singulis ad quos presentes Literæ pervenerint Edwardus Walkerus eques auratus Ordinis Periscelidis aureæ fecialis vulgò Garterus nationis Anglicanæ Armorum Rex principalis salutem. Inter cætera virtutis irritamenta, maximi profecto semper apud antecessores nostros fuere Insignia illa Armorum honoraria, quæ non tantùm viros honoratos ab ignobili plebe secernerent, sed et nobiles ipsos ad plura virtutis facinora perpetranda incitarent. Quocirca cum Gilbertus Sheldon Sacræ Theologiæ Doctor antiquâ et honoratâ Sheldonorum familiâ in agro Derbeiensi oriundus, celebri doctrina et singulari virtute nomen Majorum, per se celebre, magnoperê nobilitaverit; non modo, quod Collegium Omnium Animarum, in præclarâ Oxoniensi Academia, cui multis annis præfuit prudentissimê rexerit Caroloq; Regi memoriæ semper sacræ, ab Oratorijs privatis fuerit: necnon serenissimo domino nostro Carolo secundo (quem Deus Opt: max: diu velit incolumem) Sacelli Regii Decanum dignissimum se præstiterit: quibus omnibus sum̄a viri prudentia et gravitas semper emicuit: sed insuper quod Regis partium fidissimus fautor et adjutor, Rei-familiaris jacturam, carceres, multaq; alia seipso indignissima, maximo animo pectoreq; bene præparato pertulerit: Quibus omnibus (uti fas est) perpensis; ac etiam, quòd venerabilis ille vir Londinensis Antistes designatus est; ego præfatus Edwardus Walkerus, pro potestate mihi datâ per præfatum serenissimum Carolum Regem in fidei, meritiq; præmium et honorem, Insigne eiusdem gentilitium, viz: Tignum rubeum, tribus Cataractis argenteis impressum in Scuto ejusdem metalli, vnacum honorario additamento, Rosæ pariter argenteæ, in angulo dextro, et pro Cristâ, super galeâ et torque argenteo rubeoq; Cateractam albam, Rosam rubeam in rostro suo tenentem sicut in margine præsentium luculentius videndum est, sibi posterisq; suis gestandum præbeo (unusquisq; tamen, sub illâ differentiâ juxta leges Armorum gradui suo propriâ) semper et vbiq; prout occasio sese obtulerit, sine vindicatione. In cujus rei testimonium præsentibus nomen meum propria manu subscripsi, et Sigillum Officii mei apposui. Datis quarto die Septembris, anno regni dicti serenissimi domini nostri Caroli dei gratia magnæ Britaniæ Franciæ, et Hiberniæ Regis fidei defensoris &c. Annoq; Domini Millesimo Sexcentesimo Sexagesimo.

EDWARDUS WALKER,
Garterus, P.R.A.

[1] Paul Jodrell of Duffield, co. Derby, married in 1712, Judith, daughter and co-heir of Gilbert Sheldon, and great-niece of Gilbert Sheldon, Archbishop of Canterbury.

## *Grant of Arms to Daniel Sheldon of Ham Court, Surrey*, 1681.

To all and Singular to whom these presents shall come S^r^ William Dugdale Knt. Garter Principal King of Armes, and S^r^ Henry S^t^ George K^t^ Clarenceux King of Armes send Greeting. Whereas the R^t^ Hon^ble^ Robert Earl of Ailesbury Deputy with his Maj^ts^ approbation to His Grace Henry Duke of Norfolk Earl Marshal of England hath by Warrant or Order under his hand and the Seal of the Earle Marshall's Office bearing date the 23^th^ day of this instant December, signified unto Us That Daniel Sheldon of Ham-Court in the County of Surrey Esq^r^ (out of the great honour and respect which he bears to the memory of his deceased Uncle the Most Reverend Father in God Gilbert late Arch Bishop of Canterbury Primate and Metropolitan of all England) hath made application to him the said Deputy Earl Marshall for his Consent, That the Arms and Crest heretofore granted and assigned by S^r^ Edward Walker K^nt^ late Garter Principal King of Arms A^o^ 1660 to the said Archbishop, might be assigned and confirmed to him the said Daniel Sheldon and other the issue of Raphe Sheldon his Father elder brother to the said Arch-Bishop And Whereas y^e^ said Deputy Earl Marshall, taking into consideration That the said Arch-Bishop dying unmarried did settle his Estate upon the Issue of the said Raphe his Brother which by the death of S^r^ Joseph Sheldon K^nt^ late Alderman and sometime Lord Mayor of London, eldest Son of the said Raphe without issue male, being now devolved upon the said Daniel Sheldon Second Son of the said Raphe did thereupon Signifie unto Us his consent for our joynt assigning and confirming unto the said Daniel Sheldon, and other the issue of the said Raphe the Armes and Crest heretofore granted to the said Arch-Bishop as aforesaid Know ye therefore that we the said Garter and Clarenceux in pursuance of the Consent of the said Deputy Earl Marshall, and by authority of the Kings Letters Patents to each of us respectively granted under the Great Seal of England, have assigned and confirmed and do by these Presents assign and confirm unto the said Daniel Sheldon the Armes and Crest formerly assigned and granted by the said S^r^ Edward Walker unto the said D^r^ Gilbert Sheldon at that time designed Bishop of London but afterwards Arch-Bishop of Canterbury, Viz^t^ Argent, on a Cheveron gules three Sheldrakes of the field, with the honourable addition of a Rose Silver in a canton of the Second and for the Crest on a Wreath Argent & Gules a Sheldrake Silver holding in the beak a Rose Gules as in the margin hereof more plainly appears. To be borne and used for ever hereafter by him the said Daniel Sheldon and other the issue of Raphe Sheldon his father and the heirs and other Descendents of their bodies lawfully begotten with their due and proper differences at all times and upon all occasions according to the Law and practice of Armes without the lett interruption dispute or Contradiction of any Person or Persons whatsoever. In witness whereof we the said Garter and Clarenceux have to these presents subscribed our Names aud affixed the Seales of our respective Offices this Six and Twentieth day of December in the Three and Thirtieth year of the Reign of our Sovereign Lord Charles the Second by the Grace of God King of England Scotland France and Ireland Defender of the Faith etc^a^ Annoq, D'ni 1681.

WILLIAM DUGDALE,
Garter.

HEN: S^T^ GEORGE,
Clarenceux.

## *Grant of Arms to Dame Judith Diggs and Dame Margaret Sheldon*, 1681.

To all and singular to whom these Presents shall come S^r^ William Dugdale Kn^t^ Garter Principal King of Arms, and S^r^ Henry S^t^ George Kn^t^ Clarenceux King of Armes send Greeting. Whereas the Right Hon^ble^ Robert Earl of Ailesbury Deputy, with His Majesties approbation, to his Grace Henry Duke of Norfolk Earl Marshall of England hath by warrant or Order under his hand and the Seal of the Earl Marshalls Office bearing date the 23^th^ day of December last past, signified unto us his consent for Our Devysing, Granting and Assigning to Dame Iudith Diggs Widow of S^r^ Maurice Diggs Baronet now wife of Daniell Sheldon of Ham-Court in Com̃ Surrey Esq^r^. and to Dame Margaret Sheldon her Sister Relict of S^r^ Ioseph Sheldon K^nt^ late Alderman and sometime Lord Mayor of the City of London, daughters and coheirs of M^r^ George Rose of Eastergate in com̃ Sussex, such Armes as they and their Descendents may lawfully bear according to the Rules and practice of Armes. Know ye therefore that We the said Garter and Clarenceux in pursuance of the consent of the said Deputy Earl Marshall, and by authority of the Kings Letters Patents to each of us respectively granted under the Great Seal of England, have devysed and do by these Presents grant and assign to y^e^ said Dame Iudith and Dame Margaret the Armes hereafter mentioned Viz^t^: Ermine an Eagle displayed Sable, membered and beaked Gules, debruised with a Bendlet Componè Or and Azure, as in the margin hereof more plainly appears depicted. To be borne and used for ever hereafter by them y^e^ said Dame Iudith Diggs and Dame Margaret Sheldon and the descendents of their bodies respectively, lawfully begotten, according to the Laws, Rules and practice of Armes without the Lett Interruption dispute or contradiction of any person or persons whatsoever. In witness whereof we the said S^r^ William Dugdale Knt. Garter and S^r^ Henry S^t^ George Knt. Clarenceux Kings of Arms have to these presents subscribed our Names and affixed the Seales of our respective Offices this 16^th^ day of February in the 34^th^ year of the Reign of Our Sovereign Lord Charles the Second by the Grace of God King of England Scotl^d^ France and Ireland Defender of the Faith &c. Annoq' Domini 1681.

| WILLIAM DUGDALE, | HEN: S^T^ GEORGE, |
|---|---|
| Garter. | Clarenceux. |

## *Grant of Arms to Edward Lombe of Weston, co. Norfolk*, 1699.

To all and Singular to whom these Presents shall come, S^r^ Thomas S^t^ George, Knight, Garter Principal King of Armes and S^r^ Henry S^t^ George, Knight, Clarenceux King of Armes send greeting Whereas the most noble Prince Henry Duke of Norfolke Earl Marshal of England hath by Warrant or Order under his Hand and the Seal of His office of Earl Marshal dated the 7^th^ day of this instant February signified unto Us his consent for our Devising Granting and Assigning unto Edward Lombe of Weston in the County of Norfolke Esq^r^ High Sheriff of the said County such Armes and Crest as He and His Descendents may lawfully bear and use according to the Law and Practise of Armes, Know Ye therefore that in pursuance of the said Earl Marshals consent We the said Garter and Clarenceux by the Authority of the Letters Patents of our Offices under the great Seal of England to Us respectively Granted have Devised, Granted and Assigned and do by these Presents Devise Grant and assign for and unto the said Edward Lombe the Armes and Crest hereafter mentioned Viz^t^ Azure two Combs in Fess between a broken Lance Barrwise, one piece in Chief with the head respecting the dexter, the broken part of the other half towards the dexter base Point of the Scocheon Or, and for his Crest on a Wreath of His Colours, two Lances in Saltire Or each with a small Pendant Gules as in the Margin hereof is more plainly Depicted. To be borne and used by Him the said Edward Lombe and the Heirs and other Descendents of His Body lawfully begotten with their due and proper Differences in Shield Coat-Armour, Penon, Seal or otherwise according to the Law and due Practise of Armes without the lett or Interruption of any Person or Persons whatsoever. In Witness whereof We the said Garter and Clarenceux Kings of Armes have to these Presents subscribed Our Names and affixed the Seals of Our respective Offices this Tenth day of February in the 11^th^ year of the Reign of Our Soveraign Lord William the third by y^e^ Grace of God King of England Scotland France and Ireland Defender of the Faith &c. Annoq' D'ni Millesimo Sexcentesimo nonagesimo nono.

| | |
|---|---|
| THO. S^T^ GEORGE, Garter<br>Principall King of Armes. | HEN. S^T^ GEORGE, Clarenceux<br>King of Armes. |

---

## *Confirmation of Arms to Paul Jodrell*, 1707.

To all and Singular To whom these Presents shall come S^r^ Henry S^t^ George, Knight, Garter Principal King of Arms, and Peter Le Neve Esq^r^ Norroy King of Arms Send greeting. Whereas Paul Iodrell of Duffeild in the County of Derby Esq^r^ and Clark to the Honorable House of Commons, hath by Petition represented unto the Right Honorable Henry Earl of Bindon Deputy (with her Majesties Approbation) to his

Grace Thomas Duke of Norfolk Earl Marshall and Hereditary Marshall of England, That he is the only Son of Simon Iodrell sometime of the City of Litchfeild in the County of Stafford Deceased, who was Son of Iohn Iodrell of Litchfeild aforesaid, Second Son of the Iodrells of Moorhouse in the County of Stafford, which Iodiells of Moorhouse are Descended by a younger Son from the Ancient Family of Iodrell of Yeardesley in the County Palatine of Chester. And Whereas Edmund Iodrell of Twemlow in the said County of Chester Esq^r the present Cheif of the said Family of Yeardesley hath Certified that he doth beleive that Iohn Iodrell Second Son of Iohn Iodiell of Moorehouse in the County of Stafford Esq^r by Elizabeth Swetnam his Wife, did go and Live at the City of Litchfeild and that he might Marry Alice Iarman, from whom as he hath been credibly informed the said Paul Iodrell is Descended, and that he may be intitled to bear the Arms of the said Family of Iodrell of Moorehouse with a due distinction which (so far as concerned him) he did freely give his Consent and agree unto. And Whereas the said Paul Iodrell by the said Petition prayed to obtain the said Earl of Bindons Warrant for our Assigning and Confirming (with his Lordships consent to and Approbation thereof), the Arms and Crest of the aforesaid Family of Moorehouse with such Variation or difference as he and his Descendents may Lawfully Use and Bear. And Whereas likewise his Lordship (being well satisfied that the said Paul Iodrell is duly Qualified to Support the State of Gentility) did by Warrant under his Hand and Seal bearing date the fourteenth day of June last past Order and Appoint Us the said Garter and Norroy to Assign and Confirm to the said Paul Iodrell the Arms and Crest of the said Family with such Variation or difference as (after his Consent and Approbation thereof) may be borne and used by the said Paul Iodrell and his Descendents according to the Law of Arms. Know ye therefore that we the said Garter and Norroy in Pursuance of the said Warrant or Order and by virtue of the Letters Patents of our Offices under the Great Seal of England to each of Us respectively Granted, Have Assigned and do by these Presents Grant and Confirm unto the said Paul Iodrell (His Lordships Consent and Approbation being already had thereunto) the Arms and Crest hereafter mentioned Viz^t. Ermines three round Buckles, the Tongues downward Argent, in fess poynt a Trefoil Slipt Or, and for his Crest, on a Wreath of his Colours Argent and Sable a Cocks head and Neck Coupt, the Wings erected Or, Combed Ielloped Gules issuant out of a chaplet of Roses Gules, berded and Seeded proper as in the Margin hereof is more plainly depicted. To be borne and used by the said Paul Iodrell, and the Heirs and other Descendents of his Body Lawfully Begotten and to be Begotten, according to the Law and practice of Arms, without the Let or Interruption of any Person or Persons whatsoever. In Witness whereof we the said Garter and Norroy Kings of Arms have to these Presents Subscribed our Names and affixed the Seals of our respective Offices this Tenth day of July, in the Sixth year of the Reign of our Soveraign Lady Anne by the Grace of God Queen of Great Britain France and Ireland Defender of the Faith &c., and in the year of our Lord 1707.

HEN: S^T GEORGE, GARTER,
Principal King of Arms.

PETER LE NEVE,
Norroy King of Arms.

# *Monumental Inscriptions at Letheringsett, co. Norfolk.*

*North wall.*

IN MEMORY OF
EDWARD JODRELL ESQ$^{RE}$
OF BAYFIELD HALL IN THIS COUNTY
WHO DIED JANUARY 27$^{TH}$ 1868
AGED 54.

---

IN MEMORY OF
EDWARD JODRELL ESQ.
WHO DIED SEPTEMBER 14$^{TH}$ 1852
AGED 67 YEARS.
ALSO OF MARY HIS WIFE
WHO DIED NOVEMBER 10$^{TH}$ 1865
AGED 72 YEARS.
THIS TABLET IS ERECTED BY THEIR CHILDREN
NOT TO RECORD THEIR EXEMPLARY VIRTUES BUT AS A
TOKEN OF DEEP AND ENDURING AFFECTION.

---

TO THE MEMORY OF
HENRY JODRELL ESQ$^{RE}$
LATE OF BAYFIELD HALL IN THE COUNTY OF NORFOLK
YOUNGEST SON OF PAUL JODRELL AND ELIZABETH HIS WIFE
OF SION HILL IN THE COUNTY OF MIDDLESEX
HE WAS A BARRISTER AT LAW OF THE HON$^{BLE}$ SOCIETY OF LINCOLNS INN;
RECORDER OF GREAT YARMOUTH AND FOR SEVERAL YEARS
REPRESENTED THAT BOROUGH AND AFTERWARDS THE BOROUGH OF BRAMBER
IN PARLIAMENT.
HE DIED ON THE 11$^{TH}$ OF MARCH 1814 IN THE 63$^{D}$ YEAR OF HIS AGE
AND IS BURIED IN THE FAMILY VAULT AT LEWKNOR IN THE COUNTY OF OXFORD.
THE AFFECTION
WHICH INSCRIBED THIS TABLET, CAN BUT IMPERFECTLY EXPRESS
THE KINDNESS AND URBANITY OF HIS DOMESTIC AND SOCIAL LIFE
INTEGRITY AND USEFULNESS ADORNED
HIS PUBLIC CHARACTER.

*Arms.*—Jodrell impaling Weyland. *Crest.*—Jodrell.

---

*Under east window, north aisle, on a brass plate.*

TO THE GLORY OF GOD AND IN MOST LOVING MEMORY OF EDWARD JODRELL ESQ.
OF BAYFIELD HALL WHO DIED AT SEA MARCH 17$^{TH}$ 1882 AGED 36.
THIS WINDOW IS ERECTED BY HIS MOTHER ADELA MONCKTON JODRELL.

*Brass plate at the north side of east window.*

TO THE GLORY OF GOD AND
IN LOVING MEMORY OF EDWARD
JODRELL OF BAYFIELD HALL
THIS WINDOW IS PLACED HERE BY HIS
WIDOW ADELA MONCKTON JODRELL
ANNO DOMINI 1876.

---

*West end.*

TO GOD
THE GIVER OF ALL THINGS BE THE GLORY
AND IN MEMORY OF
LUCINDA EMMA MARIA
LADY JODRELL
THIS CHURCH WAS RE-ROOFED AND PART RE-BUILT
SHE DEPARTED THIS LIFE AT CANNES
ON MARCH 1$^{ST}$ 1888 AND
WAS BURIED IN THE FAMILY VAULT
AT LEWKNOR, OXON.
UNTIL THE DAY BREAK
AND THE SHADOWS
FLEE AWAY.

---

## IN BAYFIELD CHURCHYARD.

*North side, on a cross.*

EDWARD JODRELL
ESQUIRE
WHO DIED JANUARY 27$^{TH}$ 1868
AGED 24 YEARS.

---

## *From Fly-leaves of the Jodrell Family Bible, 1769.*

Sir John Lombe Bar$^{t}$ of Great Melton eldest Brother of Edward Hase Esq. died May 27$^{th}$ 1817.

Edward Hase Born at Dereham in the County of Norfolk Dec$^{br}$ 31 1732.

Vertue Repps Born at Matishall in the County of Norfolk June 28$^{th}$ 1732 and married Edward Hase April 16$^{th}$ 1754 at Dereham in the County of Norfolk.

*Brass plate at the north side of east window.*

TO THE GLORY OF GOD AND
IN LOVING MEMORY OF EDWARD
JODRELL OF BAYFIELD HALL
THIS WINDOW IS PLACED HERE BY HIS
WIDOW ADELA MONCKTON JODRELL
ANNO DOMINI 1876.

---

*West end.*

TO GOD
THE GIVER OF ALL THINGS BE THE GLORY
AND IN MEMORY OF
LUCINDA EMMA MARIA
LADY JODRELL
THIS CHURCH WAS RE-ROOFED AND PART RE-BUILT
SHE DEPARTED THIS LIFE AT CANNES
ON MARCH 1ST 1888 AND
WAS BURIED IN THE FAMILY VAULT
AT LEWKNOR, OXON.
UNTIL THE DAY BREAK
AND THE SHADOWS
FLEE AWAY.

---

## IN BAYFIELD CHURCHYARD.

*North side, on a cross.*

EDWARD JODRELL
ESQUIRE
WHO DIED JANUARY 27TH 1868
AGED 24 YEARS.

---

## *From Fly-leaves of the Jodrell Family Bible, 1769.*

Sir John Lombe Bart of Great Melton eldest Brother of Edward Hase Esq. died May 27th 1817.

Edward Hase Born at Dereham in the County of Norfolk Decbr 31 1732.

Vertue Repps Born at Matishall in the County of Norfolk June 28th 1732 and married Edward Hase April 16th 1754 at Dereham in the County of Norfolk.

Vertue Hase Born at Saxthorpe in the County of Norfolk May 15th 1755.
Sophia Hase Born at Saxthorpe in the County of Norfolk May 19th 1757.
Anne Hase Born at Saxthorpe in the County of Norfolk July 1st 1759.
Edward John Fountayne Hase Born at Sall in the County of Norfolk July 11th 1764. Died March 10th 1765 and buried in the Vault at Sall.
Mary Hase born at Sall in the County of Norfolk Janry 29th 1766.
Richard Paul Jodrell Born in Bedford Row in the Parish of St Andrews, London, Novbr 24th 1745 N.S. Died in Portland Place, London, Jan. 26th 1831.
Vertue Hase Born at Saxthorpe in the County of Norfolk May 15th 1755 and married Richard Paul Jodrell May 19th 1772 at Sall in the County of Norfolk. Died March 23d 1806 and buried at Lewknor, Oxon.
Paul Jodrell born in Berners Street in the Parish of Marylebone, London, March 4th 1773. Died April 12th 1774 and buried at Lewknor in in the County of Oxon.
Paul Jodrell Born in Berners Street in the Parish of Marylebone, London, April 26th 1776. Died May 10th 1776 and buried at Lewknor in the County of Oxon.
Sophia and Louisa Jodrell Born in Berners Street in the Parish of Marylebone, London, Septbr 25th 1778. Sophia died unmarried April 17th 1849 and is buried at Upton, Bucks. Louisa wife of Richard Jennings died 1826 and is buried at Ridge, Herts.
Richard Paul Jodrell Born in Berners Street in the Parish of Marylebone, London, June 26th 1781.
Edward Jodrell born in Berners Street in the Parish of Marylebone, London, Novbr 19th 1785.
Sheldon Jodrell Born in Berners Street in the Parish of Marylebone, London, August 9th 1788.
Robert Marsham Born in the Parish of St Martins in the Fields, London, December 18th 1749 N.S.
Sophia Hase Born at Saxthorpe in the County of Norfolk May the 19th 1757 and married Robert Marsham April 17th 1781 at Sall in the County of Norfolk.
Robert Marsham Born at Gunthorpe in the County of Norfolk June 24th 1783.
Sophia Vertue Marsham Born at Gunthorpe in the County of Norfolk July 8th 1784.
Lucy Marsham Born at Gunthorpe in the County of Norfolk November 6th 1786.
Edward Marsham Born at Gunthorpe in the County of Norfolk April 1st 1787.
Henry Marsham born at Saxthorpe in the County of Norfolk 13th of Novr 1788.
William George Jodrell born at 39 Manchester Street, London, on Sunday Morning May 18th 1823 baptized in Marylebone Parish Church June 16th 1823. Died Jany 20th at Sall House 1824 and Buried in Sall Vault.
Edward Repps Jodrell born at 10 Bentinck Street, London, on Monday Morning June 20th 1825 and baptized in Marylebone Parish Church July 28th 1825.

Henry Sheldon Jodrell born at 4 Bentinck Street London on Tuesday morning May 15th 1827 and baptized in Marylebone Church July 1827. Died in Portland Place Augt 9th 1832.

Richard Paul Hase Jodrell Born at 2 Duke Street Portland Place in the Parish of St Marylebone London on Monday Night Augst 3rd 1818 and baptized in Marylebone Parish Church Aug. 29th 1818 and christened in the said Church July 15th 1820.

Amelia Vertue Jodrell born also in Duke Street on Saturday Morning Decr 15th 1821 baptized in the said Church of Marylebone Janry 12th 1822.

Louisa Jodrell married Richard Jennings of Ridge, Com. Hertford Febry 12, 1811 and died July 22nd 1826.

Edward Jodrell married Mary Lowndes 4th Daughter of William Lowndes Stone Esq. of Brightwell in the County of Oxford Oct. 8th 1812.

Richard Paul Jodrell, junior married Amelia Caroline King Daughter of the Right Honourable the Earl of Kingston Decr 12th 1814 at Saint Marylebone Church London by the Honble and Revd Rich. King.

Amelia Caroline King was born and christened at Frederickton in the Province of New Brunswick in North America March 17th 1793 of which there is no record the Register of her Baptism having been destroyed by Fire.

Thomas Browne Evans born at Bury St Edmunds in the Parish of St James's in the County of Suffolk December 9th 1765.

Mary Hase Born at Sall in the County of Norfolk January 29th 1766 and Married Thomas Browne Evans January 11th 1787 at Sall in the County of Norfolk.

Thomas Browne Evans Born at Brome Place in the County of Norfolk May 31st 1789.

Edward Evans Born at Kirby Beadon in the County of Norfolk May 24th 1791.

Henry Evans born at Kirby Beadon in the County of Norfolk June the 26th 1792.

Mary Virtue Evans born at Kirby Beadon in the County of Norfolk Sept. 23d 1793.

Mary Evans wife of Thomas Brown Evans died 9th of April 1798 Aged 32.

Vertue Hase wife of Edward Hase died 25th of May 1801 Aged 69.

Edward Hase died 11th of May 1804 Aged 71.

Vertue Jodrell wife of Richard Paul Jodrell died March 23rd 1806 Aged 50.

Robert Marsham died in April 1812 Aged 62.

Sophia Marsham his Wife died Novr 28th 1824 Aged 67.

Bernard Astley third son of Sir Edward Astley Bart of Melton Constable was born August 31st 1764.

Anne Hase born at Saxthorpe July 1st 1759 married Bernard Astley August 31 1787 at Sall in the County of Norfolk.

Sir Paul Jodrell died in India 1803 at Madras.

Henry Jodrell Esq. died in Welbeck Street London March 11th 1814.

Elizabeth Lytton died in Upper Seymour Street London Novr 1, 1818.

# *Jodrell Pedigree.*

John Jodrell of Yerdesley in co. Cest[r], Esq., 2 son. = . . da: and heir of . . Beeley of Moorehouse, co. Staff: gent.

Thomas Jodrell of the Moorehouse, co. Staff: 1594. = Joane, da: and sole heir to . . Sherrat of the Lane End, within Horton Court, co. Stafford, living 27 April 1594, as appears by her son Ralph's will.

John Jodrell of the Moorehouse, co. Stafford. = Elizabeth, da: of . . Swetenham of Swetenham, co. Cestr: Esq.

Ralph Jodrell, Citizen and Pewterer of London. Will dat: 27 April, pr: 9 May 1594 (36 *Dixey*). = Margaret, da: of . . Relict and Extrix.

drell of ichfield, = Alice Jarman of City of Lichfield.

Thomas Jodrell of the Moorehouse, co. Staff: ob. 24 Dec. 1667, æt. 75. = Anne, da: of Robert Pott of Ilam, co. Staff: Esq.

Ralph. — William. — James.

Joane. — Mary.

odrell of the City eld; died before 1707. =

John Jodrell of the Moorehouse, aged 43 in 1663. = Elizabeth, da: of John Wedgwood of Harracles, co. Stafford, Esq.

Thomas. — Elizabeth. — Ursula.

rell of Duffield, in the County of Derby, the Honorable House of Commons, of the City of Lichfield, co. Stafford, he Parish of S[t] Sepulcher in the City of after that of S[t] Bride, *alias* Bridget, in the , and since the year 1689 of Chancery parish of S[t] Andrew, Holborn, co. Middle- of Sion Hill in parish of Isleworth in the nty of Middlesex; married at S[t] James', vell, 8 Jan. 1673; died 31 July 1728, aged d at Lewknor in the County of Oxford. = Jane, eldest da: of Thomas Rolles of Lewknor, co. Oxford, Esq.; died 12 Feb. 1727, æt. 78, bur[d] at Lewknor, aforesaid.

John Jodrell of the Moorehouse, æt. 18 1663. = Mary, da: of Thomas Swetenham of Bertley, co. Cestr, Esq.

Robert. — William.

Anne. — Eliza. — Hester. — Ursula.

A

Jodrell, born 20 74, bapt at S[t] e's; died in a r, and was bur[d] nor afores[d].

—

Jodrell, born 29 76, bapt. at S[t] died 16 June ried there.

Paul Jodrell, s: and h: late of Trinity Coll: Oxford, now of Lincoln's Inn, London, Esq.; born 23 June 1679; marr[d] at S[t] Edmund the King, Lombard Street, 7 Oct. 1712; ob. 25 Jan. 1744, bur[d] at Lewknor. = Judith, eld[t] of the 2 daurs. and coheirs of Gilbert Sheldon, by Mary his wife; born 12 Aug. 1692, bapt. in Hammersmith Parish; died 30 June 1768, and bur[d] at Lewknor. Mary, 2[d] da: and coh: of Gilbert Sheldon, married William Cradock of Hartforth, co. York, Esq.

B

h, 2 da: of Rich[d] Warner h Elmham, co. Norf: = Paul Jodrell of Lincoln's Inn, Esq.; born in Essex St., Strand, 20 Feb. 1713, Reg[d] in St. Clement Danes; mar. at North Elmham; ob. 30 June 1751, bur[d] at Lewknor.

Paul Jodrell, born in Bedford Row 13 Nov. pt. at S[t] Andrew's, Holborn, 29 Nov. 1745.

—

drell, born in Bedford Row 12 November pt. and reg[d] at S[t] Andrew's, Holborn.

—

Jodrell, born in Bedford Row 6 May 1750, g[d] in S[t] Andrew's, Holborn.

Elizabeth, born in Bedford Row 24 M[ch] 1747, baptism reg[d] in S[t] Andrew's, Holborn. = Rich[d] Warburton Lytton, Esq. (son of W[m] Warburton, Esq., dec[d], by Eliz: his wife, only sister of John Robinson Lytton of Knebworth, co. Hertford); marr. at S[t] Andrew's Church 16 April 1768.

*Autograph of Rev. Philip Neville Jodrell, Rector of Yelling, co. Hunts, son of Rev. Daniel Jodrell, Rector of Hingham, co. Norfolk, and Archdeacon of Rochester, by Mary his wife, daughter of Rev. John Breeze, to a letter dated Yelling Rectory, March 29th, 1848.*

*Autograph of Eliza S. Jodrell, daughter of Rev. Philip Neville Jodrell, Rector of Yelling, to a letter dated May 12th, 1846.*

A — A

James Jodrell, bapt. at S[t] Bride's; living 1707; died unm: bur[d] at Lewknor.

Richard Jodrell, bapt. at S[t] Bride's; died young, and was bur. there.

John Jodrell, bapt. at S[t] Bride's; living 1707; died unm: and bur. at Lewknor.

Rolles Jodrell, bapt. at S[t] Bride's; died young, and was bur[d] there.

Edward Jodrell, bapt. at S[t] Andrew's, Holborn; living 1707; died s.p., bur[d] at Lewknor.

Jane, born 4 July 1680, bapt. at S[t] Bride's; died young, and was bur[d] there.

Frances, bapt. at S[t] Bride's; died young, and was bur[d] there.

B — B

Thomas Jodrell, born 17 July 1716 in Essex St., and bapt. at S[t] Clement Danes; died on board the "Pelham" (Cap[t] Woodford), in service of E. I. Company when that ship was lost in Bengal River.

Daniel Jodrell, born in Essex St. in 1718, bapt. at S[t] Clement Danes. = Elizabeth, only da: of . . Breeze, Clerk, Rector of Hingham, co. Norf:

Mary, only da: of W[m] Cradock, by Mary his wife, 2[d] da: and coh: of Gilbert Sheldon; marr. at Audley St. Chapel 9 Dec. 1740; ob. 12 March 1745, æt. 26, bur[d] at Lewknor. 1st wife. = Gilbert Jodrell of Ankerwycke, died 1772. = Ann, 2[d] da: of Samuel Vanderplank of Tokenhouse Yard, London, a Blackwell Hall Factor, by Hannah his wife; marr. at Whitehall Chapel 28 June 1747. 2nd wife.

Sarah, born in Chancery Lane 23 Sept. 1741, bapt. by the Rector of St. Andrew's, Holborn; marr. in psh Church of Wraysbury, co. Bucks, 6 Oct. 1763. = Robert Child, Esq., only surviving son of Samuel Child, Esq. (by Agatha his wife), only surviving son of Sir Francis Child, Knt., formerly Lord Mayor of London.

Sarah Anne, born in Lincoln's Inn Fields 28 Aug. 1764, bapt. and reg[d] in S[t] Giles in the Fields, co. Midd[x]; marr., 20 May 1782, John, 10th Earl of Westmoreland, K.G., died 9 November 1793.

Ann, born in Bedford Row 28 Jan. 174$\frac{8}{9}$, bapt. by the Rector of S[t] Andrew's, Holborn.

Hannah, born in Bedford Row 19 M[ch] 1749, bapt. by Rector of S[t] Andrew's, Holborn; died the same month, and bur[d] at S[t] Andrew's.

Letitia Elizabeth, born in Bedford Row 29 May 1751, bapt. by Rector of S[t] Andrew's, Holborn; died at Bath 10 July 1760, bur[d] at Lewknor.

A

Francis Nourse of Woodeaton, co. Oxford; died 5 Dec. 1732, burd there 6th. = Anne, 4 da: bapt. at St Bride's; burd 11 Sept. 1728 at Woodeaton.

Henry Jodrell of Trin: Coll: Oxford, bapt. at St Bride's; burd at Isleworth, co. Middx. = Mary, da: of . . Davenport of Isleworth; died March 1768, burd at Isleworth.

Elizabeth, eldt da: born 6 June 1677, bapt. at St Bride's; marr. at Isleworth July 1700; burd at Bledlow. = Henry Shallcross (son and heir of John Shallcross of Bledlow, co. Bucks, Esq.); died . . burd at Bledlow.

Mary, born at Ickenham, co. Middx; marr. Robt Shorditch of same place, Esq.

John Ansell of Brentford, co. Middx; marr. at Ickenham. = Jane, born at Ickenham.

Elizabeth, born at Ickenham; living unmarried.

John born at Brentford, co. Middx.

Jane, born at Brentford.

[Sh]eldon Jod[re]ll, born in [E]ssex St. June [..]25, bapt. at [St] Clement [Da]nes; ob. [..] Feb. 1727, [bu]rd at Lewk[no]r.

Philip Jodrell, born in Essex St. 30 April 1722, bapt. at St Clement Danes; marr. at Rolvenden, Kent, 8 June 1761; ob. 14 Feb. 1763, and burd there s.p. = Eliza: da: of Philips Gybbon of Rolvenden, co. Kent, Esq.

Lydia Catherine, born in Essex St. 16 Mch 1722, bapt. at St Clement Danes; ob. 8 Sept. 1724, burd at Ealing, co. Middx.

Elizabeth, born in Essex St. 24 Mch 1720; bapt. at St Clement Danes; marr. at Woodeaton, co. Oxon, 16 Oct. 1744, John Morton of Tackley, co. Oxford, Chief Justice of County of Chester.

Judith, born in Essex St. 19 Jan. 1717, bapt. at St. Clement Danes, marr. at Ickenham, co. Middx, 16 July 1739; burd at Woodeaton 22 March 1759. = John Nourse of Woodeaton, co. Oxon, Esq., born in St Andrew's, Holborn, 25, and bapt. 30 Nov. 1710.

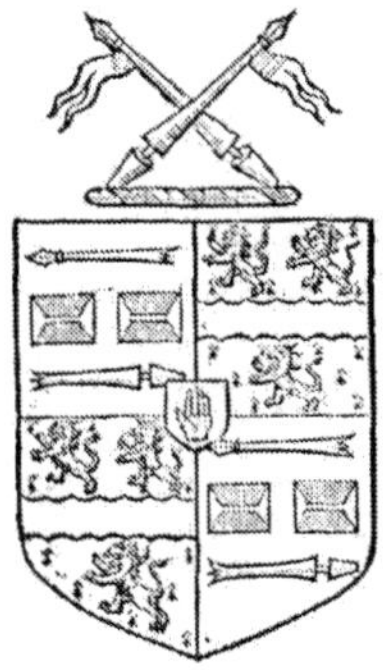

*Arms.*—Quarterly, 1 and 4, Lombe; 2 and 3, Hase.

# *Pedigree of Lombe, Hase, and Jodrell.*

(FROM THE RECORDS OF THE COLLEGE OF ARMS.)

Edward Lombe of Weston in the County of Norfolk, Esq.

Edward Lombe of Great Melton, co. Norfolk; ob: s.p. in April 1738.

John Lombe of Great Melton, afores^d, clerk; ob: s.p.

Mary Lombe, sister and heir by will of her brother John; died about 1776, bur^d at Great Melton. = John Hase of Great Melton, co. Norfolk, Esq., bur^d at Great Melton.

John Hase of Great Melton, co. Norfolk, Esq., born about 1731. Assumed the name of Lombe only; unmarried in 1783.

Edward Hase of Sall in co. Norfolk, born about 1733; marr. at Dereham in said County in April 1754; now living. = Vertue, 3^d and youngest daughter and coheir of John Repps of Mattishall, co. Norfolk, Esq., living 1783.

Richard Paul Jodrell of Duffield, co. Derby, and of Saxlingham, co. Norfolk, eldest son and heir of Paul Jodrell, Esq.; born in the parish of S^t Andrew's, Holborn, 13 Nov. 1745. = Vertue Hase, eld^t da: born at Saxthorpe, co. Norfolk, 15 May 1755; marr. 19 May 1772 at Sall aforesaid.

Edward Hase, only son, died an infant.

—

Sophia, born 19 May 1757 at Saxthorpe; marr^d in April 1781 to Robert Marsham of Stratton, co. Norf^k, Esq.

Anne, born 1 July 1759 at Saxthorpe; living unmarried.

—

Mary.

Paul Jodrell, born 4 M^ch 1773.

—

Paul Jodrell, born 26 April 1775.

—

Both died infants, bur^d at Lewknor, co. Oxon.

Richard Paul Jodrell, born 26 June 1781 in parish of S^t Marylebone.

Sophia and Louisa (twins), born 25 Sept. 1778 in the parish of S^t Marylebone.

*The above pedigree of our Families is true to the best of our knowledge and Belief. Witness our Hands at the College of Arms this 13 Day of December 1783.*

Richard Paul Jodrell

Vertue Jodrell

# *Pedigree of Rev. Sir Edward Repps Jodrell, Bart.*

Paul Jodrell of Duffield, co. Derby (son of Paul Jodrell of London, by Judith his wife, dau. and coheir of Gilbert Sheldon, and great-niece of Gilbert Sheldon, Archbishop of Canterbury); born 20 February 1713; of Trinity College, Oxford, matriculated 7 November 1730, aged 15, created M.A. 22 February 1732, Barrister-at-Law of Lincoln's Inn 1735, Solicitor-General to Frederick, Prince of Wales, M.P. for Old Sarum January 1751; died 30 June 1751. = Elizabeth, dau. of Richard Warner of North Elmham, co. Norfolk, by Elizabeth his wife, dau. of Edward Lombe of Weston, co. Norfolk.

A

Richard Paul Jodrell, born 24 November 1745; of Hertford College, Oxford, matriculated 28 June 1764, aged 18, created D.C.L. 4 July 1793, Barrister-at-Law of Lincoln's Inn 1771, F.R.S. 1772, F.S.A. 1784, M.P. for Seaford, co. Sussex, 1790–96; died at Portland Place, London, 26 January 1831. = Vertue, eldest dau. and coheir of Edward Hase of Sall, co. Norfolk, by Vertue his wife, youngest dau. and coheir of John Repps of Mattishall, co. Norfolk; born at Saxthorpe, co. Norfolk, 15 May 1755; marr. at Sall 19 May 1772; died, aged 50, 23 March 1806, bur. at Lewknor, co. Oxford.

Sir Paul Jodrell of St. John's College, Cambridge, B.A. 1769, M.A. 1772, M.D. 1786, knighted 26 October 1787; Physician to the Nabob of Arcot; died at Madras in 1803. = Jane dau. of Sir Robert Bewicke of Close House, co. Northumberland, by Mary his wife, dau. of Robert Hurst of Nottingham.

Paulina Elizabeth, marr. 4 June 1804, Sir John Henry Seale, Bart., of Mount Boone, co. Devon (son of John Seale of Mount Boone, by Sarah his wife, dau. of Charles Hayne of Lupton); born in August 1785; M.P. for Dartmouth; created a Baronet 31 July 1838; died 29 November 1844. She died 17 April 1862.

B

Paul Jodrell, born in Berners Street, London, 4 March 1773; died 12 April 1774, bur. at Lewknor.

Paul Jodrell, born in Berners Street, London, 26 April 1776; died 10 May 1776, bur. at Lewknor.

Sophia (twin with Louisa), born in Berners Street, London 25 September 1778; died 17 April 1849, bur. at Upton, co. Bucks.

Louisa (twin with Sophia), born in Berners Street, London, 25 September 1778; marr. 12 February 1811, Richards Jennings of Gellydeg, co. Carmarthen. She died 22 July 1826, and was bur. at Ridge, co. Herts.

Sir Richard Paul Jodrell, 2nd Bart. (succeeded on the death of his great uncle, Sir John Lombe [formerly Hase], unmarr. 27 May 1817); born in Berners Street, London, 26 June 1781; of Magdalen College, Oxford, matriculated 1 July 1799, aged 18, B.A. 1804, M.A. 1806, Barrister-at-Law of Lincoln's Inn 1803; died 14 January 1861. = Amelia Caroline King, illegitimate dau. of Robert, 2nd Earl of Kingston; born at Frederickton, New Brunswick, 17 March 1793, bapt. there privately the same day; marr. at St. Marylebone, London, 12 Dec. 1814; died 18 Jan. 1860.

C

Richard Paul Hase Jodrell, born in Duke Street, Portland Place, London, 3 August, bapt. at St. Marylebone 29 Aug. 1818; of New College, Oxford, matriculated 13 January 1836, aged 17; died 12 November 1855. = Lady Anna Maria Isabella Moore, dau. of Stephen, 3rd Earl of Mountcashell, by Anna Maria his wife, dau. of Samuel Wyss of Berne, Switzerland; marr. 27 July 1848. She marr. 2ndly, 30 April 1856, James Herbert Freme of Wrentnall House, co. Salop.

A

Henry Jodrell of Bayfield Hall, Holt, co. Norfolk; Barrister-at-Law of Lincoln's Inn, Recorder of Great Yarmouth, M.P. for the same place, and afterwards of Bramber; died, aged 63, 11 March 1814, bur. at Lewknor.

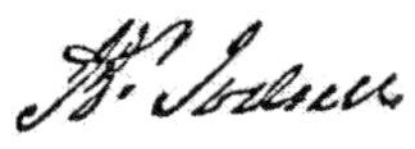


= Johanna Elizabeth, eldest dau. of John Weyland of Woodrising and Woodeaton, co. Oxford; marr. 2 September 1807. She marr. 2ndly, 20 July 1815, George N. Best of the Middle Temple, Barrister-at-Law, who died, aged 76, 25 March 1845.

Elizabeth, marr. in 1768 to Richard Warburton Lytton of Knebworth, co. Herts, who died 29 December 1810, having had an only dau. and heir, Elizabeth Barbara of Knebworth, who, by Royal Licence dated 25 November 1811, took the surname and Arms of Lytton, in addition to, and after that of Bulwer, she having marr., 1 June 1798, Brigadier-General William Earle Bulwer of Wood Dalling and Heydon, co. Norfolk, who was born 22 March 1757, and was bur. 14 July 1807. She died 19 December 1844.

B

Edward Jodrell, born in Berners Street, London, 19 November, bapt. at St. Marylebone 17 December 1785; of Trinity College, Oxford, matriculated 17 May 1804, aged 18, B.A. 1808, M.A. 1811; died, aged 67, 14 September, bur. at Bracon Ash, co. Norfolk, 21 September 1852. M.I.

= Mary, 5th dau. of William and Elizabeth Lowndes Stone of Brightwell Park, co. Oxford; born at Brightwell 4 February, bapt. there 6 March 1793; marr. at Brightwell 8 October 1812, died, aged 72, 10 November, bur. at Marcham, co. Berks, 14 November 1865.

Rev. Sheldon Jodrell, born in Berners Street, London, 9 August 1788; of Trinity College, Cambridge, B.A. 1812, M.A. 1815.

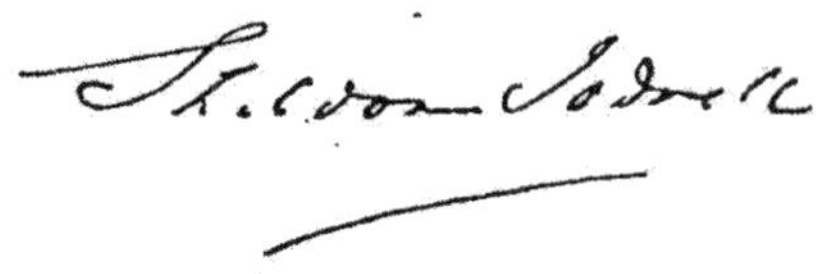


*(For issue see "Visitation of England and Wales," Vol. I., page 33.)*

C

William George Jodrell, born at 39 Manchester Street, London, Sunday morning, 18 May, bapt. at Marylebone Parish Church 16 June 1823; died at Sall House 20 January 1824, bur. at Sall.

Rev. Sir Edward Repps Jodrell, born at 10 Bentinck Street, London, Monday morning, 20 June, bapt. at Marylebone Parish Church 28 July 1825; of Queen's College, Oxford, matriculated 1 February 1843, aged 17, B.A. of New Inn Hall 1848, M.A. of Queen's College 1849; Rector of Saxlingham, co. Norfolk, 1855–61; died 12 November 1882.

= Lucinda Emma Maria, dau. of Robert Theophilus Garden of River Lyons, King's County, Ireland; marr. 10 June 1852; died at Cannes, aged 63, 1 March 1888, bur. at Lewknor.

Henry Sheldon Jodrell, born at 4 Bentinck St., London, 15 May, bapt. at St. Marylebone in July 1827; died at Portland Place, London, 9 August 1832.

Amelia Vertue, born in Duke Street, Portland Place, 29 Dec. 1821, bapt. at St. Marylebone 12 Jan. 1822; marr. 18 June 1842; assumed, by Royal Licence dated 1883, the surname and arms of Jodrell; died, aged 68, 15 Sept., bur. in Brompton Cemetery, London, 22 Sept. 1890.

= Charles Fitzgerald Higgins of Westport, co. Mayo, Ireland (son of Captain Fitzgerald Higgins of Westport, J.P., by Mary his wife, dau. of William Ouseley of Rushbrook); born 31 July 1815; J.P. for co. Mayo; died in July 1860.

Richard George Higgins, born 11 November 1843.

Frederick Palisser Higgins, born 16 September 1853; died 4 January, bur. in Brompton Cemetery 9 January 1854.

Emily Vertue Jane, marr. 3 June 1871.

= Herbert Henry Churchill, assumed by Royal Licence, dated 31 March 1883, the surname and Arms of Jodrell in lieu of that of Churchill.

JOHN REPPS

NON SIBI SED PATRIÆ NATUS

SOPHIA, LOUISA, AND SHELDON JODRELL,
CHILDREN OF RICHARD PAUL JODRELL, BY VERTUE HIS WIFE, ELDEST
DAUGHTER AND COHEIR OF EDWARD HASE OF SALL, NORFOLK

PLAN OF THE FAMILY VAULT IN THE NORTH AISLE OF SALL CHURCH.



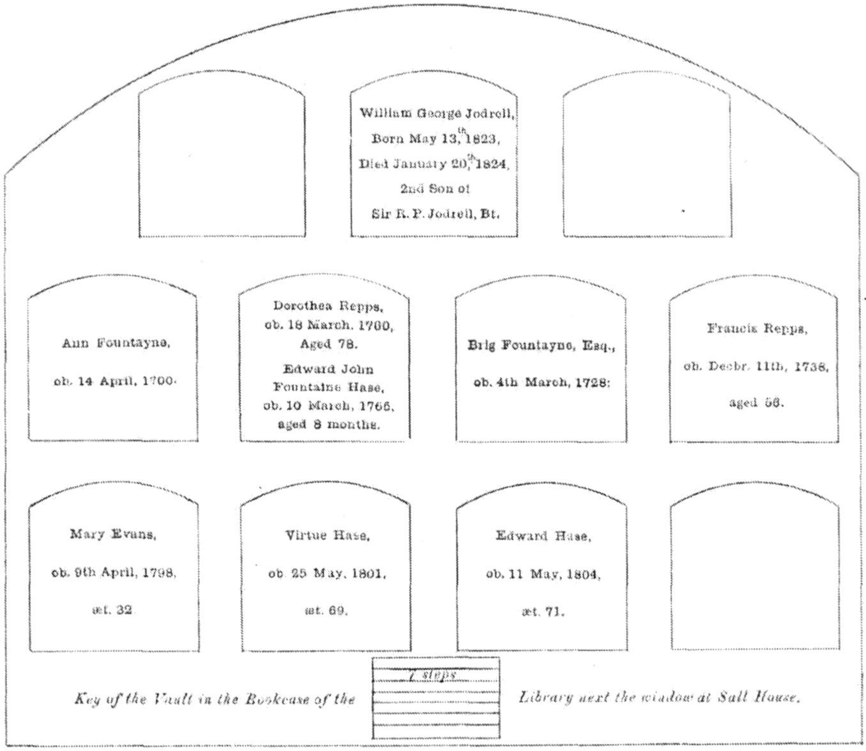


*The Vault is 12 feet square from the bottom of the steps to the 11 niches, and 7½ feet high, and each niche about 7 feet long.*

COPIED FROM A DRAWING INSERTED IN AN OLD BIBLE BELONGING TO SIR ALFRED JODRELL, BART.

# INDEX.

# INDEX.

Lightning Source UK Ltd.
Milton Keynes UK
UKHW021617171022
410614UK00007B/1462